Password Compendium

For the Heart of Faith

A Vale Removed Book

ISBN: 978-1-970509-00-7
Printed in the United States of America
First Edition, 2025

May the Lord bless you in everything you do.

"Before I formed you in the womb I knew you."

Jeremiah 1:5

At-a-Glance Passwords

Website ______________________________
Username ______________________________
Email ______________________________
Password ______________________________
Password Update ______________________________
Password Update ______________________________
Password Hint 1) ______________ 2) ______________
Customer ID ______________ Security Pin ______________
Date ______________ Note ______________

Website ______________________________
Username ______________________________
Email ______________________________
Password ______________________________
Password Update ______________________________
Password Update ______________________________
Password Hint 1) ______________ 2) ______________
Customer ID ______________ Security Pin ______________
Date ______________ Note ______________

Website ______________________________
Username ______________________________
Email ______________________________
Password ______________________________
Password Update ______________________________
Password Update ______________________________
Password Hint 1) ______________ 2) ______________
Customer ID ______________ Security Pin ______________
Date ______________ Note ______________

At-a-Glance Passwords

Website ____________________
Username ____________________
Email ____________________
Password ____________________
Password Update ____________________
Password Update ____________________
Password Hint 1) ____________ 2) ____________
Customer ID ____________ Security Pin ____________
Date ____________ Note ____________

Website ____________________
Username ____________________
Email ____________________
Password ____________________
Password Update ____________________
Password Update ____________________
Password Hint 1) ____________ 2) ____________
Customer ID ____________ Security Pin ____________
Date ____________ Note ____________

Website ____________________
Username ____________________
Email ____________________
Password ____________________
Password Update ____________________
Password Update ____________________
Password Hint 1) ____________ 2) ____________
Customer ID ____________ Security Pin ____________
Date ____________ Note ____________

At-a-Glance Passwords

Website ______________________________

Username ______________________________

Email ______________________________

Password ______________________________

Password Update ______________________________

Password Update ______________________________

Password Hint 1) ______________ 2) ______________

Customer ID ______________ Security Pin ______________

Date ______________ Note ______________

Website ______________________________

Username ______________________________

Email ______________________________

Password ______________________________

Password Update ______________________________

Password Update ______________________________

Password Hint 1) ______________ 2) ______________

Customer ID ______________ Security Pin ______________

Date ______________ Note ______________

Website ______________________________

Username ______________________________

Email ______________________________

Password ______________________________

Password Update ______________________________

Password Update ______________________________

Password Hint 1) ______________ 2) ______________

Customer ID ______________ Security Pin ______________

Date ______________ Note ______________

At-a-Glance Passwords

Website

Username

Email

Password

Password Update

Password Update

Password Hint 1) 2)

Customer ID Security Pin

Date Note

Website

Username

Email

Password

Password Update

Password Update

Password Hint 1) 2)

Customer ID Security Pin

Date Note

Website

Username

Email

Password

Password Update

Password Update

Password Hint 1) 2)

Customer ID Security Pin

Date Note

At-a-Glance Passwords

Website ____________________
Username ____________________
Email ____________________
Password ____________________
Password Update ____________________
Password Update ____________________
Password Hint 1) ____________ 2) ____________
Customer ID ____________ Security Pin ____________
Date ____________ Note ____________

Website ____________________
Username ____________________
Email ____________________
Password ____________________
Password Update ____________________
Password Update ____________________
Password Hint 1) ____________ 2) ____________
Customer ID ____________ Security Pin ____________
Date ____________ Note ____________

Website ____________________
Username ____________________
Email ____________________
Password ____________________
Password Update ____________________
Password Update ____________________
Password Hint 1) ____________ 2) ____________
Customer ID ____________ Security Pin ____________
Date ____________ Note ____________

At-a-Glance Passwords

Website

Username

Email

Password

Password Update

Password Update

Password Hint 1) 2)

Customer ID Security Pin

Date Note

Website

Username

Email

Password

Password Update

Password Update

Password Hint 1) 2)

Customer ID Security Pin

Date Note

Website

Username

Email

Password

Password Update

Password Update

Password Hint 1) 2)

Customer ID Security Pin

Date Note

"My grace is sufficient for you, for power is perfected in weakness."

2 Corinthians 12:9

A

Website
Username
Email
Password
Password Update
Password Update
Password Hint 1) 2)
Customer ID Security Pin
Date Note

Website
Username
Email
Password
Password Update
Password Update
Password Hint 1) 2)
Customer ID Security Pin
Date Note

Website
Username
Email
Password
Password Update
Password Update
Password Hint 1) 2)
Customer ID Security Pin
Date Note

A

Website

Username

Email

Password

Password Update

Password Update

Password Hint 1) 2)

Customer ID Security Pin

Date Note

Website

Username

Email

Password

Password Update

Password Update

Password Hint 1) 2)

Customer ID Security Pin

Date Note

Website

Username

Email

Password

Password Update

Password Update

Password Hint 1) 2)

Customer ID Security Pin

Date Note

A

Website
Username
Email
Password
Password Update
Password Update
Password Hint 1) 2)
Customer ID Security Pin
Date Note

Website
Username
Email
Password
Password Update
Password Update
Password Hint 1) 2)
Customer ID Security Pin
Date Note

Website
Username
Email
Password
Password Update
Password Update
Password Hint 1) 2)
Customer ID Security Pin
Date Note

A

Website

Username

Email

Password

Password Update

Password Update

Password Hint 1) 2)

Customer ID Security Pin

Date Note

Website

Username

Email

Password

Password Update

Password Update

Password Hint 1) 2)

Customer ID Security Pin

Date Note

Website

Username

Email

Password

Password Update

Password Update

Password Hint 1) 2)

Customer ID Security Pin

Date Note

A

Website
Username
Email
Password
Password Update
Password Update
Password Hint 1) 2)
Customer ID Security Pin
Date Note

Website
Username
Email
Password
Password Update
Password Update
Password Hint 1) 2)
Customer ID Security Pin
Date Note

Website
Username
Email
Password
Password Update
Password Update
Password Hint 1) 2)
Customer ID Security Pin
Date Note

A

Website
Username
Email
Password
Password Update
Password Update
Password Hint 1) 2)
Customer ID Security Pin
Date Note

Website
Username
Email
Password
Password Update
Password Update
Password Hint 1) 2)
Customer ID Security Pin
Date Note

Website
Username
Email
Password
Password Update
Password Update
Password Hint 1) 2)
Customer ID Security Pin
Date Note

"Do not be conformed to this world, but be transformed by the renewing of your mind, so that you may prove what the will of God is, that which is good and acceptable and perfect."

Romans 12:2

B

Website

Username

Email

Password

Password Update

Password Update

Password Hint 1) 2)

Customer ID Security Pin

Date Note

Website

Username

Email

Password

Password Update

Password Update

Password Hint 1) 2)

Customer ID Security Pin

Date Note

Website

Username

Email

Password

Password Update

Password Update

Password Hint 1) 2)

Customer ID Security Pin

Date Note

B

Website

Username

Email

Password

Password Update

Password Update

Password Hint 1) 2)

Customer ID Security Pin

Date Note

Website

Username

Email

Password

Password Update

Password Update

Password Hint 1) 2)

Customer ID Security Pin

Date Note

Website

Username

Email

Password

Password Update

Password Update

Password Hint 1) 2)

Customer ID Security Pin

Date Note

B

Website

Username

Email

Password

Password Update

Password Update

Password Hint 1) 2)

Customer ID Security Pin

Date Note

Website

Username

Email

Password

Password Update

Password Update

Password Hint 1) 2)

Customer ID Security Pin

Date Note

Website

Username

Email

Password

Password Update

Password Update

Password Hint 1) 2)

Customer ID Security Pin

Date Note

B

Website

Username

Email

Password

Password Update

Password Update

Password Hint 1) 2)

Customer ID Security Pin

Date Note

Website

Username

Email

Password

Password Update

Password Update

Password Hint 1) 2)

Customer ID Security Pin

Date Note

Website

Username

Email

Password

Password Update

Password Update

Password Hint 1) 2)

Customer ID Security Pin

Date Note

B

Website
Username
Email
Password
Password Update
Password Update
Password Hint 1) 2)
Customer ID Security Pin
Date Note

Website
Username
Email
Password
Password Update
Password Update
Password Hint 1) 2)
Customer ID Security Pin
Date Note

Website
Username
Email
Password
Password Update
Password Update
Password Hint 1) 2)
Customer ID Security Pin
Date Note

B

Website

Username

Email

Password

Password Update

Password Update

Password Hint 1) 2)

Customer ID Security Pin

Date Note

Website

Username

Email

Password

Password Update

Password Update

Password Hint 1) 2)

Customer ID Security Pin

Date Note

Website

Username

Email

Password

Password Update

Password Update

Password Hint 1) 2)

Customer ID Security Pin

Date Note

"Where your treasure is,
there your heart will be also."

Matthew 6:21

Website

Username

Email

Password

Password Update

Password Update

Password Hint 1) 2)

Customer ID Security Pin

Date Note

Website

Username

Email

Password

Password Update

Password Update

Password Hint 1) 2)

Customer ID Security Pin

Date Note

Website

Username

Email

Password

Password Update

Password Update

Password Hint 1) 2)

Customer ID Security Pin

Date Note

C

Website

Username

Email

Password

Password Update

Password Update

Password Hint 1) 2)

Customer ID Security Pin

Date Note

Website

Username

Email

Password

Password Update

Password Update

Password Hint 1) 2)

Customer ID Security Pin

Date Note

Website

Username

Email

Password

Password Update

Password Update

Password Hint 1) 2)

Customer ID Security Pin

Date Note

C

Website

Username

Email

Password

Password Update

Password Update

Password Hint 1) 2)

Customer ID Security Pin

Date Note

Website

Username

Email

Password

Password Update

Password Update

Password Hint 1) 2)

Customer ID Security Pin

Date Note

Website

Username

Email

Password

Password Update

Password Update

Password Hint 1) 2)

Customer ID Security Pin

Date Note

C

Website

Username

Email

Password

Password Update

Password Update

Password Hint 1) 2)

Customer ID Security Pin

Date Note

Website

Username

Email

Password

Password Update

Password Update

Password Hint 1) 2)

Customer ID Security Pin

Date Note

Website

Username

Email

Password

Password Update

Password Update

Password Hint 1) 2)

Customer ID Security Pin

Date Note

Website
Username
Email
Password
Password Update
Password Update
Password Hint 1) 2)
Customer ID Security Pin
Date Note

Website
Username
Email
Password
Password Update
Password Update
Password Hint 1) 2)
Customer ID Security Pin
Date Note

Website
Username
Email
Password
Password Update
Password Update
Password Hint 1) 2)
Customer ID Security Pin
Date Note

C

Website

Username

Email

Password

Password Update

Password Update

Password Hint 1) 2)

Customer ID Security Pin

Date Note

Website

Username

Email

Password

Password Update

Password Update

Password Hint 1) 2)

Customer ID Security Pin

Date Note

Website

Username

Email

Password

Password Update

Password Update

Password Hint 1) 2)

Customer ID Security Pin

Date Note

"Come to Me, all who are weary and heavy-laden, and I will give you rest. Take My yoke upon you and learn from Me, for I am gentle and humble in heart, and YOU WILL FIND REST FOR YOUR SOULS. For My yoke is easy and My burden is light."

Matthew 11:28-30

Website

Username

Email

Password

Password Update

Password Update

Password Hint 1) 2)

Customer ID Security Pin

Date Note

Website

Username

Email

Password

Password Update

Password Update

Password Hint 1) 2)

Customer ID Security Pin

Date Note

Website

Username

Email

Password

Password Update

Password Update

Password Hint 1) 2)

Customer ID Security Pin

Date Note

D

Website
Username
Email
Password
Password Update
Password Update
Password Hint 1) 2)
Customer ID Security Pin
Date Note

Website
Username
Email
Password
Password Update
Password Update
Password Hint 1) 2)
Customer ID Security Pin
Date Note

Website
Username
Email
Password
Password Update
Password Update
Password Hint 1) 2)
Customer ID Security Pin
Date Note

Website

Username

Email

Password

Password Update

Password Update

Password Hint 1) 2)

Customer ID Security Pin

Date Note

Website

Username

Email

Password

Password Update

Password Update

Password Hint 1) 2)

Customer ID Security Pin

Date Note

Website

Username

Email

Password

Password Update

Password Update

Password Hint 1) 2)

Customer ID Security Pin

Date Note

D

Website

Username

Email

Password

Password Update

Password Update

Password Hint 1) 2)

Customer ID Security Pin

Date Note

Website

Username

Email

Password

Password Update

Password Update

Password Hint 1) 2)

Customer ID Security Pin

Date Note

Website

Username

Email

Password

Password Update

Password Update

Password Hint 1) 2)

Customer ID Security Pin

Date Note

Website
Username
Email
Password
Password Update
Password Update
Password Hint 1) 2)
Customer ID Security Pin
Date Note

Website
Username
Email
Password
Password Update
Password Update
Password Hint 1) 2)
Customer ID Security Pin
Date Note

Website
Username
Email
Password
Password Update
Password Update
Password Hint 1) 2)
Customer ID Security Pin
Date Note

D

Website

Username

Email

Password

Password Update

Password Update

Password Hint 1) 2)

Customer ID Security Pin

Date Note

Website

Username

Email

Password

Password Update

Password Update

Password Hint 1) 2)

Customer ID Security Pin

Date Note

Website

Username

Email

Password

Password Update

Password Update

Password Hint 1) 2)

Customer ID Security Pin

Date Note

"The LORD has looked down from heaven upon the sons of men to see if there are any who understand, who seek after God."

Psalms 14:2

E

Website
Username
Email
Password
Password Update
Password Update
Password Hint 1) 2)
Customer ID Security Pin
Date Note

Website
Username
Email
Password
Password Update
Password Update
Password Hint 1) 2)
Customer ID Security Pin
Date Note

Website
Username
Email
Password
Password Update
Password Update
Password Hint 1) 2)
Customer ID Security Pin
Date Note

E

Website

Username

Email

Password

Password Update

Password Update

Password Hint 1) 2)

Customer ID Security Pin

Date Note

Website

Username

Email

Password

Password Update

Password Update

Password Hint 1) 2)

Customer ID Security Pin

Date Note

Website

Username

Email

Password

Password Update

Password Update

Password Hint 1) 2)

Customer ID Security Pin

Date Note

Website
Username
Email
Password
Password Update
Password Update
Password Hint 1) 2)
Customer ID Security Pin
Date Note

Website
Username
Email
Password
Password Update
Password Update
Password Hint 1) 2)
Customer ID Security Pin
Date Note

Website
Username
Email
Password
Password Update
Password Update
Password Hint 1) 2)
Customer ID Security Pin
Date Note

E

Website

Username

Email

Password

Password Update

Password Update

Password Hint 1) 2)

Customer ID Security Pin

Date Note

Website

Username

Email

Password

Password Update

Password Update

Password Hint 1) 2)

Customer ID Security Pin

Date Note

Website

Username

Email

Password

Password Update

Password Update

Password Hint 1) 2)

Customer ID Security Pin

Date Note

Website
Username
Email
Password
Password Update
Password Update
Password Hint 1) 2)
Customer ID Security Pin
Date Note

Website
Username
Email
Password
Password Update
Password Update
Password Hint 1) 2)
Customer ID Security Pin
Date Note

Website
Username
Email
Password
Password Update
Password Update
Password Hint 1) 2)
Customer ID Security Pin
Date Note

E

Website

Username

Email

Password

Password Update

Password Update

Password Hint 1) 2)

Customer ID Security Pin

Date Note

Website

Username

Email

Password

Password Update

Password Update

Password Hint 1) 2)

Customer ID Security Pin

Date Note

Website

Username

Email

Password

Password Update

Password Update

Password Hint 1) 2)

Customer ID Security Pin

Date Note

"For the eyes of the LORD move to and fro throughout the earth that He may strongly support those whose heart is completely His."

2 Chronicles 16:9

Website

Username

Email

Password

Password Update

Password Update

Password Hint 1) 2)

Customer ID Security Pin

Date Note

Website

Username

Email

Password

Password Update

Password Update

Password Hint 1) 2)

Customer ID Security Pin

Date Note

Website

Username

Email

Password

Password Update

Password Update

Password Hint 1) 2)

Customer ID Security Pin

Date Note

F

Website

Username

Email

Password

Password Update

Password Update

Password Hint 1) 2)

Customer ID Security Pin

Date Note

Website

Username

Email

Password

Password Update

Password Update

Password Hint 1) 2)

Customer ID Security Pin

Date Note

Website

Username

Email

Password

Password Update

Password Update

Password Hint 1) 2)

Customer ID Security Pin

Date Note

Website
Username
Email
Password
Password Update
Password Update
Password Hint 1) 2)
Customer ID Security Pin
Date Note

Website
Username
Email
Password
Password Update
Password Update
Password Hint 1) 2)
Customer ID Security Pin
Date Note

Website
Username
Email
Password
Password Update
Password Update
Password Hint 1) 2)
Customer ID Security Pin
Date Note

F

Website
Username
Email
Password
Password Update
Password Update
Password Hint 1) 2)
Customer ID Security Pin
Date Note

Website
Username
Email
Password
Password Update
Password Update
Password Hint 1) 2)
Customer ID Security Pin
Date Note

Website
Username
Email
Password
Password Update
Password Update
Password Hint 1) 2)
Customer ID Security Pin
Date Note

Website
Username
Email
Password
Password Update
Password Update
Password Hint 1) 2)
Customer ID Security Pin
Date Note

Website
Username
Email
Password
Password Update
Password Update
Password Hint 1) 2)
Customer ID Security Pin
Date Note

Website
Username
Email
Password
Password Update
Password Update
Password Hint 1) 2)
Customer ID Security Pin
Date Note

F

Website

Username

Email

Password

Password Update

Password Update

Password Hint 1) 2)

Customer ID Security Pin

Date Note

Website

Username

Email

Password

Password Update

Password Update

Password Hint 1) 2)

Customer ID Security Pin

Date Note

Website

Username

Email

Password

Password Update

Password Update

Password Hint 1) 2)

Customer ID Security Pin

Date Note

"Stand firm therefore, having girded your loins with truth, and having put on the breastplate of righteousness, and having shod your feed with the preparation of the Gospel of Peace."

Ephesians 6:14-15

Website

Username

Email

Password

Password Update

Password Update

Password Hint 1) 2)

Customer ID Security Pin

Date Note

Website

Username

Email

Password

Password Update

Password Update

Password Hint 1) 2)

Customer ID Security Pin

Date Note

Website

Username

Email

Password

Password Update

Password Update

Password Hint 1) 2)

Customer ID Security Pin

Date Note

G

Website

Username

Email

Password

Password Update

Password Update

Password Hint 1) 2)

Customer ID Security Pin

Date Note

Website

Username

Email

Password

Password Update

Password Update

Password Hint 1) 2)

Customer ID Security Pin

Date Note

Website

Username

Email

Password

Password Update

Password Update

Password Hint 1) 2)

Customer ID Security Pin

Date Note

Website
Username
Email
Password
Password Update
Password Update
Password Hint 1) 2)
Customer ID Security Pin
Date Note

Website
Username
Email
Password
Password Update
Password Update
Password Hint 1) 2)
Customer ID Security Pin
Date Note

Website
Username
Email
Password
Password Update
Password Update
Password Hint 1) 2)
Customer ID Security Pin
Date Note

G

Website ____________________
Username ____________________
Email ____________________
Password ____________________
Password Update ____________________
Password Update ____________________
Password Hint 1) ____________ 2) ____________
Customer ID ____________ Security Pin ____________
Date ____________ Note ____________

Website ____________________
Username ____________________
Email ____________________
Password ____________________
Password Update ____________________
Password Update ____________________
Password Hint 1) ____________ 2) ____________
Customer ID ____________ Security Pin ____________
Date ____________ Note ____________

Website ____________________
Username ____________________
Email ____________________
Password ____________________
Password Update ____________________
Password Update ____________________
Password Hint 1) ____________ 2) ____________
Customer ID ____________ Security Pin ____________
Date ____________ Note ____________

Website
Username
Email
Password
Password Update
Password Update
Password Hint 1) 2)
Customer ID Security Pin
Date Note

Website
Username
Email
Password
Password Update
Password Update
Password Hint 1) 2)
Customer ID Security Pin
Date Note

Website
Username
Email
Password
Password Update
Password Update
Password Hint 1) 2)
Customer ID Security Pin
Date Note

G

Website ______

Username ______

Email ______

Password ______

Password Update ______

Password Update ______

Password Hint 1) ______ 2) ______

Customer ID ______ Security Pin ______

Date ______ Note ______

Website ______

Username ______

Email ______

Password ______

Password Update ______

Password Update ______

Password Hint 1) ______ 2) ______

Customer ID ______ Security Pin ______

Date ______ Note ______

Website ______

Username ______

Email ______

Password ______

Password Update ______

Password Update ______

Password Hint 1) ______ 2) ______

Customer ID ______ Security Pin ______

Date ______ Note ______

"Then Peter came and said to Him, 'Lord, how often shall my brother sin against me and I forgive him? Up to seven times?' Jesus *said to him, 'I do not say to you, up to seven times, but up to seventy times seven.'"

Matthew 18:21-22

H

Website
Username
Email
Password
Password Update
Password Update
Password Hint 1) 2)
Customer ID Security Pin
Date Note

Website
Username
Email
Password
Password Update
Password Update
Password Hint 1) 2)
Customer ID Security Pin
Date Note

Website
Username
Email
Password
Password Update
Password Update
Password Hint 1) 2)
Customer ID Security Pin
Date Note

H

Website
Username
Email
Password
Password Update
Password Update
Password Hint 1) 2)
Customer ID Security Pin
Date Note

Website
Username
Email
Password
Password Update
Password Update
Password Hint 1) 2)
Customer ID Security Pin
Date Note

Website
Username
Email
Password
Password Update
Password Update
Password Hint 1) 2)
Customer ID Security Pin
Date Note

H

Website
Username
Email
Password
Password Update
Password Update
Password Hint 1) 2)
Customer ID Security Pin
Date Note

Website
Username
Email
Password
Password Update
Password Update
Password Hint 1) 2)
Customer ID Security Pin
Date Note

Website
Username
Email
Password
Password Update
Password Update
Password Hint 1) 2)
Customer ID Security Pin
Date Note

H

Website

Username

Email

Password

Password Update

Password Update

Password Hint 1) 2)

Customer ID Security Pin

Date Note

Website

Username

Email

Password

Password Update

Password Update

Password Hint 1) 2)

Customer ID Security Pin

Date Note

Website

Username

Email

Password

Password Update

Password Update

Password Hint 1) 2)

Customer ID Security Pin

Date Note

H

Website

Username

Email

Password

Password Update

Password Update

Password Hint 1) 2)

Customer ID Security Pin

Date Note

Website

Username

Email

Password

Password Update

Password Update

Password Hint 1) 2)

Customer ID Security Pin

Date Note

Website

Username

Email

Password

Password Update

Password Update

Password Hint 1) 2)

Customer ID Security Pin

Date Note

H

Website

Username

Email

Password

Password Update

Password Update

Password Hint 1) 2)

Customer ID Security Pin

Date Note

Website

Username

Email

Password

Password Update

Password Update

Password Hint 1) 2)

Customer ID Security Pin

Date Note

Website

Username

Email

Password

Password Update

Password Update

Password Hint 1) 2)

Customer ID Security Pin

Date Note

"Therefore, I am well content with weaknesses, with insults, with distresses, with persecutions, with difficulties, for Christ's sake; for when I am weak, then I am strong."

2 Corinthians 12:10

Website

Username

Email

Password

Password Update

Password Update

Password Hint 1) 2)

Customer ID Security Pin

Date Note

Website

Username

Email

Password

Password Update

Password Update

Password Hint 1) 2)

Customer ID Security Pin

Date Note

Website

Username

Email

Password

Password Update

Password Update

Password Hint 1) 2)

Customer ID Security Pin

Date Note

I

Website

Username

Email

Password

Password Update

Password Update

Password Hint 1) 2)

Customer ID Security Pin

Date Note

Website

Username

Email

Password

Password Update

Password Update

Password Hint 1) 2)

Customer ID Security Pin

Date Note

Website

Username

Email

Password

Password Update

Password Update

Password Hint 1) 2)

Customer ID Security Pin

Date Note

Website

Username

Email

Password

Password Update

Password Update

Password Hint 1) 2)

Customer ID Security Pin

Date Note

Website

Username

Email

Password

Password Update

Password Update

Password Hint 1) 2)

Customer ID Security Pin

Date Note

Website

Username

Email

Password

Password Update

Password Update

Password Hint 1) 2)

Customer ID Security Pin

Date Note

I

Website

Username

Email

Password

Password Update

Password Update

Password Hint 1) 2)

Customer ID Security Pin

Date Note

Website

Username

Email

Password

Password Update

Password Update

Password Hint 1) 2)

Customer ID Security Pin

Date Note

Website

Username

Email

Password

Password Update

Password Update

Password Hint 1) 2)

Customer ID Security Pin

Date Note

Website
Username
Email
Password
Password Update
Password Update
Password Hint 1) 2)
Customer ID Security Pin
Date Note

Website
Username
Email
Password
Password Update
Password Update
Password Hint 1) 2)
Customer ID Security Pin
Date Note

Website
Username
Email
Password
Password Update
Password Update
Password Hint 1) 2)
Customer ID Security Pin
Date Note

I

Website
Username
Email
Password
Password Update
Password Update
Password Hint 1) 2)
Customer ID Security Pin
Date Note

Website
Username
Email
Password
Password Update
Password Update
Password Hint 1) 2)
Customer ID Security Pin
Date Note

Website
Username
Email
Password
Password Update
Password Update
Password Hint 1) 2)
Customer ID Security Pin
Date Note

"For the mouth speaks out
of that which fills the heart."

Matthew 12:34

Website
Username
Email
Password
Password Update
Password Update
Password Hint 1) 2)
Customer ID Security Pin
Date Note

Website
Username
Email
Password
Password Update
Password Update
Password Hint 1) 2)
Customer ID Security Pin
Date Note

Website
Username
Email
Password
Password Update
Password Update
Password Hint 1) 2)
Customer ID Security Pin
Date Note

J

Website

Username

Email

Password

Password Update

Password Update

Password Hint 1) 2)

Customer ID Security Pin

Date Note

Website

Username

Email

Password

Password Update

Password Update

Password Hint 1) 2)

Customer ID Security Pin

Date Note

Website

Username

Email

Password

Password Update

Password Update

Password Hint 1) 2)

Customer ID Security Pin

Date Note

Website

Username

Email

Password

Password Update

Password Update

Password Hint 1) 2)

Customer ID Security Pin

Date Note

Website

Username

Email

Password

Password Update

Password Update

Password Hint 1) 2)

Customer ID Security Pin

Date Note

Website

Username

Email

Password

Password Update

Password Update

Password Hint 1) 2)

Customer ID Security Pin

Date Note

J

Website
Username
Email
Password
Password Update
Password Update
Password Hint 1) 2)
Customer ID Security Pin
Date Note

Website
Username
Email
Password
Password Update
Password Update
Password Hint 1) 2)
Customer ID Security Pin
Date Note

Website
Username
Email
Password
Password Update
Password Update
Password Hint 1) 2)
Customer ID Security Pin
Date Note

Website

Username

Email

Password

Password Update

Password Update

Password Hint 1) 2)

Customer ID Security Pin

Date Note

Website

Username

Email

Password

Password Update

Password Update

Password Hint 1) 2)

Customer ID Security Pin

Date Note

Website

Username

Email

Password

Password Update

Password Update

Password Hint 1) 2)

Customer ID Security Pin

Date Note

J

Website

Username

Email

Password

Password Update

Password Update

Password Hint 1) 2)

Customer ID Security Pin

Date Note

Website

Username

Email

Password

Password Update

Password Update

Password Hint 1) 2)

Customer ID Security Pin

Date Note

Website

Username

Email

Password

Password Update

Password Update

Password Hint 1) 2)

Customer ID Security Pin

Date Note

"And we know that God causes all things to work together for good to those who love God, to those who are called according to His purpose."

Romans 8:28

Website

Username

Email

Password

Password Update

Password Update

Password Hint 1) 2)

Customer ID Security Pin

Date Note

Website

Username

Email

Password

Password Update

Password Update

Password Hint 1) 2)

Customer ID Security Pin

Date Note

Website

Username

Email

Password

Password Update

Password Update

Password Hint 1) 2)

Customer ID Security Pin

Date Note

K

Website

Username

Email

Password

Password Update

Password Update

Password Hint 1) 2)

Customer ID Security Pin

Date Note

Website

Username

Email

Password

Password Update

Password Update

Password Hint 1) 2)

Customer ID Security Pin

Date Note

Website

Username

Email

Password

Password Update

Password Update

Password Hint 1) 2)

Customer ID Security Pin

Date Note

Website
Username
Email
Password
Password Update
Password Update
Password Hint 1) 2)
Customer ID Security Pin
Date Note

Website
Username
Email
Password
Password Update
Password Update
Password Hint 1) 2)
Customer ID Security Pin
Date Note

Website
Username
Email
Password
Password Update
Password Update
Password Hint 1) 2)
Customer ID Security Pin
Date Note

K

Website

Username

Email

Password

Password Update

Password Update

Password Hint 1) 2)

Customer ID Security Pin

Date Note

Website

Username

Email

Password

Password Update

Password Update

Password Hint 1) 2)

Customer ID Security Pin

Date Note

Website

Username

Email

Password

Password Update

Password Update

Password Hint 1) 2)

Customer ID Security Pin

Date Note

Website

Username

Email

Password

Password Update

Password Update

Password Hint 1) 2)

Customer ID Security Pin

Date Note

Website

Username

Email

Password

Password Update

Password Update

Password Hint 1) 2)

Customer ID Security Pin

Date Note

Website

Username

Email

Password

Password Update

Password Update

Password Hint 1) 2)

Customer ID Security Pin

Date Note

K

Website

Username

Email

Password

Password Update

Password Update

Password Hint 1) 2)

Customer ID Security Pin

Date Note

Website

Username

Email

Password

Password Update

Password Update

Password Hint 1) 2)

Customer ID Security Pin

Date Note

Website

Username

Email

Password

Password Update

Password Update

Password Hint 1) 2)

Customer ID Security Pin

Date Note

"For God has not given us a spirit of timidity,
but of power and love and discipline."

2 Timothy 1:7

Website
Username
Email
Password
Password Update
Password Update
Password Hint 1) 2)
Customer ID Security Pin
Date Note

Website
Username
Email
Password
Password Update
Password Update
Password Hint 1) 2)
Customer ID Security Pin
Date Note

Website
Username
Email
Password
Password Update
Password Update
Password Hint 1) 2)
Customer ID Security Pin
Date Note

L

Website

Username

Email

Password

Password Update

Password Update

Password Hint 1) 2)

Customer ID Security Pin

Date Note

Website

Username

Email

Password

Password Update

Password Update

Password Hint 1) 2)

Customer ID Security Pin

Date Note

Website

Username

Email

Password

Password Update

Password Update

Password Hint 1) 2)

Customer ID Security Pin

Date Note

Website

Username

Email

Password

Password Update

Password Update

Password Hint 1) 2)

Customer ID Security Pin

Date Note

Website

Username

Email

Password

Password Update

Password Update

Password Hint 1) 2)

Customer ID Security Pin

Date Note

Website

Username

Email

Password

Password Update

Password Update

Password Hint 1) 2)

Customer ID Security Pin

Date Note

L

Website

Username

Email

Password

Password Update

Password Update

Password Hint 1) 2)

Customer ID Security Pin

Date Note

Website

Username

Email

Password

Password Update

Password Update

Password Hint 1) 2)

Customer ID Security Pin

Date Note

Website

Username

Email

Password

Password Update

Password Update

Password Hint 1) 2)

Customer ID Security Pin

Date Note

L

Website
Username
Email
Password
Password Update
Password Update
Password Hint 1) 2)
Customer ID Security Pin
Date Note

Website
Username
Email
Password
Password Update
Password Update
Password Hint 1) 2)
Customer ID Security Pin
Date Note

Website
Username
Email
Password
Password Update
Password Update
Password Hint 1) 2)
Customer ID Security Pin
Date Note

L

Website ______

Username ______

Email ______

Password ______

Password Update ______

Password Update ______

Password Hint 1) ______ 2) ______

Customer ID ______ Security Pin ______

Date ______ Note ______

Website ______

Username ______

Email ______

Password ______

Password Update ______

Password Update ______

Password Hint 1) ______ 2) ______

Customer ID ______ Security Pin ______

Date ______ Note ______

Website ______

Username ______

Email ______

Password ______

Password Update ______

Password Update ______

Password Hint 1) ______ 2) ______

Customer ID ______ Security Pin ______

Date ______ Note ______

"Go home to your people and report to them what great things the Lord has done for you, and how He had mercy on you."

Mark 5:19

M

Website
Username
Email
Password
Password Update
Password Update
Password Hint 1) 2)
Customer ID Security Pin
Date Note

Website
Username
Email
Password
Password Update
Password Update
Password Hint 1) 2)
Customer ID Security Pin
Date Note

Website
Username
Email
Password
Password Update
Password Update
Password Hint 1) 2)
Customer ID Security Pin
Date Note

M

Website

Username

Email

Password

Password Update

Password Update

Password Hint 1) 2)

Customer ID Security Pin

Date Note

Website

Username

Email

Password

Password Update

Password Update

Password Hint 1) 2)

Customer ID Security Pin

Date Note

Website

Username

Email

Password

Password Update

Password Update

Password Hint 1) 2)

Customer ID Security Pin

Date Note

Website

Username

Email

Password

Password Update

Password Update

Password Hint 1) 2)

Customer ID Security Pin

Date Note

Website

Username

Email

Password

Password Update

Password Update

Password Hint 1) 2)

Customer ID Security Pin

Date Note

Website

Username

Email

Password

Password Update

Password Update

Password Hint 1) 2)

Customer ID Security Pin

Date Note

M

Website

Username

Email

Password

Password Update

Password Update

Password Hint 1) 2)

Customer ID Security Pin

Date Note

Website

Username

Email

Password

Password Update

Password Update

Password Hint 1) 2)

Customer ID Security Pin

Date Note

Website

Username

Email

Password

Password Update

Password Update

Password Hint 1) 2)

Customer ID Security Pin

Date Note

Website
Username
Email
Password
Password Update
Password Update
Password Hint 1) 2)
Customer ID Security Pin
Date Note

Website
Username
Email
Password
Password Update
Password Update
Password Hint 1) 2)
Customer ID Security Pin
Date Note

Website
Username
Email
Password
Password Update
Password Update
Password Hint 1) 2)
Customer ID Security Pin
Date Note

M

Website
Username
Email
Password
Password Update
Password Update
Password Hint 1) 2)
Customer ID Security Pin
Date Note

Website
Username
Email
Password
Password Update
Password Update
Password Hint 1) 2)
Customer ID Security Pin
Date Note

Website
Username
Email
Password
Password Update
Password Update
Password Hint 1) 2)
Customer ID Security Pin
Date Note

"I have learned to be content in whatever circumstances I am. I know how to get along with humble means, and I also know how to live in prosperity; in any and every circumstance I have learned the secret of being filled and going hungry, both of having abundance and suffering need. I can do all things through Him who strengthens me."

Philippians 4:11-13

N

Website
Username
Email
Password
Password Update
Password Update
Password Hint 1) 2)
Customer ID Security Pin
Date Note

Website
Username
Email
Password
Password Update
Password Update
Password Hint 1) 2)
Customer ID Security Pin
Date Note

Website
Username
Email
Password
Password Update
Password Update
Password Hint 1) 2)
Customer ID Security Pin
Date Note

N

Website

Username

Email

Password

Password Update

Password Update

Password Hint 1) 2)

Customer ID Security Pin

Date Note

Website

Username

Email

Password

Password Update

Password Update

Password Hint 1) 2)

Customer ID Security Pin

Date Note

Website

Username

Email

Password

Password Update

Password Update

Password Hint 1) 2)

Customer ID Security Pin

Date Note

Website

Username

Email

Password

Password Update

Password Update

Password Hint 1) 2)

Customer ID Security Pin

Date Note

Website

Username

Email

Password

Password Update

Password Update

Password Hint 1) 2)

Customer ID Security Pin

Date Note

Website

Username

Email

Password

Password Update

Password Update

Password Hint 1) 2)

Customer ID Security Pin

Date Note

N

Website

Username

Email

Password

Password Update

Password Update

Password Hint 1) 2)

Customer ID Security Pin

Date Note

Website

Username

Email

Password

Password Update

Password Update

Password Hint 1) 2)

Customer ID Security Pin

Date Note

Website

Username

Email

Password

Password Update

Password Update

Password Hint 1) 2)

Customer ID Security Pin

Date Note

Website

Username

Email

Password

Password Update

Password Update

Password Hint 1) 2)

Customer ID Security Pin

Date Note

Website

Username

Email

Password

Password Update

Password Update

Password Hint 1) 2)

Customer ID Security Pin

Date Note

Website

Username

Email

Password

Password Update

Password Update

Password Hint 1) 2)

Customer ID Security Pin

Date Note

N

Website

Username

Email

Password

Password Update

Password Update

Password Hint 1) 2)

Customer ID Security Pin

Date Note

Website

Username

Email

Password

Password Update

Password Update

Password Hint 1) 2)

Customer ID Security Pin

Date Note

Website

Username

Email

Password

Password Update

Password Update

Password Hint 1) 2)

Customer ID Security Pin

Date Note

"Therefore if anyone is in Christ, he is a new creature; the old things passed away; behold, new things have come."

2 Corinthians 5:17-18

Website
Username
Email
Password
Password Update
Password Update
Password Hint 1) 2)
Customer ID Security Pin
Date Note

Website
Username
Email
Password
Password Update
Password Update
Password Hint 1) 2)
Customer ID Security Pin
Date Note

Website
Username
Email
Password
Password Update
Password Update
Password Hint 1) 2)
Customer ID Security Pin
Date Note

O

Website

Username

Email

Password

Password Update

Password Update

Password Hint 1) 2)

Customer ID Security Pin

Date Note

Website

Username

Email

Password

Password Update

Password Update

Password Hint 1) 2)

Customer ID Security Pin

Date Note

Website

Username

Email

Password

Password Update

Password Update

Password Hint 1) 2)

Customer ID Security Pin

Date Note

Website

Username

Email

Password

Password Update

Password Update

Password Hint 1) 2)

Customer ID Security Pin

Date Note

Website

Username

Email

Password

Password Update

Password Update

Password Hint 1) 2)

Customer ID Security Pin

Date Note

Website

Username

Email

Password

Password Update

Password Update

Password Hint 1) 2)

Customer ID Security Pin

Date Note

O

Website

Username

Email

Password

Password Update

Password Update

Password Hint 1) 2)

Customer ID Security Pin

Date Note

Website

Username

Email

Password

Password Update

Password Update

Password Hint 1) 2)

Customer ID Security Pin

Date Note

Website

Username

Email

Password

Password Update

Password Update

Password Hint 1) 2)

Customer ID Security Pin

Date Note

Website
Username
Email
Password
Password Update
Password Update
Password Hint 1) 2)
Customer ID Security Pin
Date Note

Website
Username
Email
Password
Password Update
Password Update
Password Hint 1) 2)
Customer ID Security Pin
Date Note

Website
Username
Email
Password
Password Update
Password Update
Password Hint 1) 2)
Customer ID Security Pin
Date Note

O

Website
Username
Email
Password
Password Update
Password Update
Password Hint 1) 2)
Customer ID Security Pin
Date Note

Website
Username
Email
Password
Password Update
Password Update
Password Hint 1) 2)
Customer ID Security Pin
Date Note

Website
Username
Email
Password
Password Update
Password Update
Password Hint 1) 2)
Customer ID Security Pin
Date Note

"The Son of Man did not come to be served, but to serve, and to give His life a ransom for many."

Matthew 20:28

Website
Username
Email
Password
Password Update
Password Update
Password Hint 1) 2)
Customer ID Security Pin
Date Note

Website
Username
Email
Password
Password Update
Password Update
Password Hint 1) 2)
Customer ID Security Pin
Date Note

Website
Username
Email
Password
Password Update
Password Update
Password Hint 1) 2)
Customer ID Security Pin
Date Note

P

Website

Username

Email

Password

Password Update

Password Update

Password Hint 1) 2)

Customer ID Security Pin

Date Note

Website

Username

Email

Password

Password Update

Password Update

Password Hint 1) 2)

Customer ID Security Pin

Date Note

Website

Username

Email

Password

Password Update

Password Update

Password Hint 1) 2)

Customer ID Security Pin

Date Note

Website

Username

Email

Password

Password Update

Password Update

Password Hint 1) 2)

Customer ID Security Pin

Date Note

Website

Username

Email

Password

Password Update

Password Update

Password Hint 1) 2)

Customer ID Security Pin

Date Note

Website

Username

Email

Password

Password Update

Password Update

Password Hint 1) 2)

Customer ID Security Pin

Date Note

P

Website

Username

Email

Password

Password Update

Password Update

Password Hint 1) 2)

Customer ID Security Pin

Date Note

Website

Username

Email

Password

Password Update

Password Update

Password Hint 1) 2)

Customer ID Security Pin

Date Note

Website

Username

Email

Password

Password Update

Password Update

Password Hint 1) 2)

Customer ID Security Pin

Date Note

Website
Username
Email
Password
Password Update
Password Update
Password Hint 1) 2)
Customer ID Security Pin
Date Note

Website
Username
Email
Password
Password Update
Password Update
Password Hint 1) 2)
Customer ID Security Pin
Date Note

Website
Username
Email
Password
Password Update
Password Update
Password Hint 1) 2)
Customer ID Security Pin
Date Note

P

Website
Username
Email
Password
Password Update
Password Update
Password Hint 1) 2)
Customer ID Security Pin
Date Note

Website
Username
Email
Password
Password Update
Password Update
Password Hint 1) 2)
Customer ID Security Pin
Date Note

Website
Username
Email
Password
Password Update
Password Update
Password Hint 1) 2)
Customer ID Security Pin
Date Note

"If anyone wishes to come after Me,
he must deny himself, and take up
his cross and follow Me."

Matthew 16:24

Q

Website

Username

Email

Password

Password Update

Password Update

Password Hint 1) 2)

Customer ID Security Pin

Date Note

Website

Username

Email

Password

Password Update

Password Update

Password Hint 1) 2)

Customer ID Security Pin

Date Note

Website

Username

Email

Password

Password Update

Password Update

Password Hint 1) 2)

Customer ID Security Pin

Date Note

Q

Website

Username

Email

Password

Password Update

Password Update

Password Hint 1) 2)

Customer ID Security Pin

Date Note

Website

Username

Email

Password

Password Update

Password Update

Password Hint 1) 2)

Customer ID Security Pin

Date Note

Website

Username

Email

Password

Password Update

Password Update

Password Hint 1) 2)

Customer ID Security Pin

Date Note

Q

Website

Username

Email

Password

Password Update

Password Update

Password Hint 1) 2)

Customer ID Security Pin

Date Note

Website

Username

Email

Password

Password Update

Password Update

Password Hint 1) 2)

Customer ID Security Pin

Date Note

Website

Username

Email

Password

Password Update

Password Update

Password Hint 1) 2)

Customer ID Security Pin

Date Note

Q

Website

Username

Email

Password

Password Update

Password Update

Password Hint 1) 2)

Customer ID Security Pin

Date Note

Website

Username

Email

Password

Password Update

Password Update

Password Hint 1) 2)

Customer ID Security Pin

Date Note

Website

Username

Email

Password

Password Update

Password Update

Password Hint 1) 2)

Customer ID Security Pin

Date Note

Website ____________________
Username ____________________
Email ____________________
Password ____________________
Password Update ____________________
Password Update ____________________
Password Hint 1) ____________ 2) ____________
Customer ID ____________ Security Pin ____________
Date ____________ Note ____________

Website ____________________
Username ____________________
Email ____________________
Password ____________________
Password Update ____________________
Password Update ____________________
Password Hint 1) ____________ 2) ____________
Customer ID ____________ Security Pin ____________
Date ____________ Note ____________

Website ____________________
Username ____________________
Email ____________________
Password ____________________
Password Update ____________________
Password Update ____________________
Password Hint 1) ____________ 2) ____________
Customer ID ____________ Security Pin ____________
Date ____________ Note ____________

Q

Website
Username
Email
Password
Password Update
Password Update
Password Hint 1) 2)
Customer ID Security Pin
Date Note

Website
Username
Email
Password
Password Update
Password Update
Password Hint 1) 2)
Customer ID Security Pin
Date Note

Website
Username
Email
Password
Password Update
Password Update
Password Hint 1) 2)
Customer ID Security Pin
Date Note

"Therefore, we are ambassadors for Christ,
as though God were making an appeal
through us; we beg you on behalf of Christ,
be reconciled to God."

2 Corinthians 5:20

Website

Username

Email

Password

Password Update

Password Update

Password Hint 1) 2)

Customer ID Security Pin

Date Note

Website

Username

Email

Password

Password Update

Password Update

Password Hint 1) 2)

Customer ID Security Pin

Date Note

Website

Username

Email

Password

Password Update

Password Update

Password Hint 1) 2)

Customer ID Security Pin

Date Note

R

Website

Username

Email

Password

Password Update

Password Update

Password Hint 1) 2)

Customer ID Security Pin

Date Note

Website

Username

Email

Password

Password Update

Password Update

Password Hint 1) 2)

Customer ID Security Pin

Date Note

Website

Username

Email

Password

Password Update

Password Update

Password Hint 1) 2)

Customer ID Security Pin

Date Note

R

Website

Username

Email

Password

Password Update

Password Update

Password Hint 1) 2)

Customer ID Security Pin

Date Note

Website

Username

Email

Password

Password Update

Password Update

Password Hint 1) 2)

Customer ID Security Pin

Date Note

Website

Username

Email

Password

Password Update

Password Update

Password Hint 1) 2)

Customer ID Security Pin

Date Note

R

Website

Username

Email

Password

Password Update

Password Update

Password Hint 1) 2)

Customer ID Security Pin

Date Note

Website

Username

Email

Password

Password Update

Password Update

Password Hint 1) 2)

Customer ID Security Pin

Date Note

Website

Username

Email

Password

Password Update

Password Update

Password Hint 1) 2)

Customer ID Security Pin

Date Note

Website

Username

Email

Password

Password Update

Password Update

Password Hint 1) 2)

Customer ID Security Pin

Date Note

Website

Username

Email

Password

Password Update

Password Update

Password Hint 1) 2)

Customer ID Security Pin

Date Note

Website

Username

Email

Password

Password Update

Password Update

Password Hint 1) 2)

Customer ID Security Pin

Date Note

R

Website

Username

Email

Password

Password Update

Password Update

Password Hint 1) 2)

Customer ID Security Pin

Date Note

Website

Username

Email

Password

Password Update

Password Update

Password Hint 1) 2)

Customer ID Security Pin

Date Note

Website

Username

Email

Password

Password Update

Password Update

Password Hint 1) 2)

Customer ID Security Pin

Date Note

"The LORD is near to the brokenhearted
and saves those who are crushed in spirit."

Psalms 34:18

S

Website

Username

Email

Password

Password Update

Password Update

Password Hint 1) 2)

Customer ID Security Pin

Date Note

Website

Username

Email

Password

Password Update

Password Update

Password Hint 1) 2)

Customer ID Security Pin

Date Note

Website

Username

Email

Password

Password Update

Password Update

Password Hint 1) 2)

Customer ID Security Pin

Date Note

S

Website

Username

Email

Password

Password Update

Password Update

Password Hint 1) 2)

Customer ID Security Pin

Date Note

Website

Username

Email

Password

Password Update

Password Update

Password Hint 1) 2)

Customer ID Security Pin

Date Note

Website

Username

Email

Password

Password Update

Password Update

Password Hint 1) 2)

Customer ID Security Pin

Date Note

Website

Username

Email

Password

Password Update

Password Update

Password Hint 1) 2)

Customer ID Security Pin

Date Note

Website

Username

Email

Password

Password Update

Password Update

Password Hint 1) 2)

Customer ID Security Pin

Date Note

Website

Username

Email

Password

Password Update

Password Update

Password Hint 1) 2)

Customer ID Security Pin

Date Note

S

Website
Username
Email
Password
Password Update
Password Update
Password Hint 1) 2)
Customer ID Security Pin
Date Note

Website
Username
Email
Password
Password Update
Password Update
Password Hint 1) 2)
Customer ID Security Pin
Date Note

Website
Username
Email
Password
Password Update
Password Update
Password Hint 1) 2)
Customer ID Security Pin
Date Note

S

Website

Username

Email

Password

Password Update

Password Update

Password Hint 1) 2)

Customer ID Security Pin

Date Note

Website

Username

Email

Password

Password Update

Password Update

Password Hint 1) 2)

Customer ID Security Pin

Date Note

Website

Username

Email

Password

Password Update

Password Update

Password Hint 1) 2)

Customer ID Security Pin

Date Note

S

Website

Username

Email

Password

Password Update

Password Update

Password Hint 1) 2)

Customer ID Security Pin

Date Note

Website

Username

Email

Password

Password Update

Password Update

Password Hint 1) 2)

Customer ID Security Pin

Date Note

Website

Username

Email

Password

Password Update

Password Update

Password Hint 1) 2)

Customer ID Security Pin

Date Note

"Yet those who wait for the LORD will gain new strength; they will mount up with wings like eagles, they will run and not get tired, they will walk and not become weary."

Isaiah 40:31

T

Website

Username

Email

Password

Password Update

Password Update

Password Hint 1) 2)

Customer ID Security Pin

Date Note

Website

Username

Email

Password

Password Update

Password Update

Password Hint 1) 2)

Customer ID Security Pin

Date Note

Website

Username

Email

Password

Password Update

Password Update

Password Hint 1) 2)

Customer ID Security Pin

Date Note

T

Website

Username

Email

Password

Password Update

Password Update

Password Hint 1) 2)

Customer ID Security Pin

Date Note

Website

Username

Email

Password

Password Update

Password Update

Password Hint 1) 2)

Customer ID Security Pin

Date Note

Website

Username

Email

Password

Password Update

Password Update

Password Hint 1) 2)

Customer ID Security Pin

Date Note

Website
Username
Email
Password
Password Update
Password Update
Password Hint 1) 2)
Customer ID Security Pin
Date Note

Website
Username
Email
Password
Password Update
Password Update
Password Hint 1) 2)
Customer ID Security Pin
Date Note

Website
Username
Email
Password
Password Update
Password Update
Password Hint 1) 2)
Customer ID Security Pin
Date Note

T

Website
Username
Email
Password
Password Update
Password Update
Password Hint 1) 2)
Customer ID Security Pin
Date Note

Website
Username
Email
Password
Password Update
Password Update
Password Hint 1) 2)
Customer ID Security Pin
Date Note

Website
Username
Email
Password
Password Update
Password Update
Password Hint 1) 2)
Customer ID Security Pin
Date Note

Website

Username

Email

Password

Password Update

Password Update

Password Hint 1) 2)

Customer ID Security Pin

Date Note

Website

Username

Email

Password

Password Update

Password Update

Password Hint 1) 2)

Customer ID Security Pin

Date Note

Website

Username

Email

Password

Password Update

Password Update

Password Hint 1) 2)

Customer ID Security Pin

Date Note

T

Website

Username

Email

Password

Password Update

Password Update

Password Hint 1) 2)

Customer ID Security Pin

Date Note

Website

Username

Email

Password

Password Update

Password Update

Password Hint 1) 2)

Customer ID Security Pin

Date Note

Website

Username

Email

Password

Password Update

Password Update

Password Hint 1) 2)

Customer ID Security Pin

Date Note

"The gifts and the calling of God are irrevocable."

Romans 11:29

Website
Username
Email
Password
Password Update
Password Update
Password Hint 1) 2)
Customer ID Security Pin
Date Note

Website
Username
Email
Password
Password Update
Password Update
Password Hint 1) 2)
Customer ID Security Pin
Date Note

Website
Username
Email
Password
Password Update
Password Update
Password Hint 1) 2)
Customer ID Security Pin
Date Note

U

Website

Username

Email

Password

Password Update

Password Update

Password Hint 1) 2)

Customer ID Security Pin

Date Note

Website

Username

Email

Password

Password Update

Password Update

Password Hint 1) 2)

Customer ID Security Pin

Date Note

Website

Username

Email

Password

Password Update

Password Update

Password Hint 1) 2)

Customer ID Security Pin

Date Note

Website
Username
Email
Password
Password Update
Password Update
Password Hint 1) 2)
Customer ID Security Pin
Date Note

Website
Username
Email
Password
Password Update
Password Update
Password Hint 1) 2)
Customer ID Security Pin
Date Note

Website
Username
Email
Password
Password Update
Password Update
Password Hint 1) 2)
Customer ID Security Pin
Date Note

U

Website

Username

Email

Password

Password Update

Password Update

Password Hint 1) 2)

Customer ID Security Pin

Date Note

Website

Username

Email

Password

Password Update

Password Update

Password Hint 1) 2)

Customer ID Security Pin

Date Note

Website

Username

Email

Password

Password Update

Password Update

Password Hint 1) 2)

Customer ID Security Pin

Date Note

Website
Username
Email
Password
Password Update
Password Update
Password Hint 1) 2)
Customer ID Security Pin
Date Note

Website
Username
Email
Password
Password Update
Password Update
Password Hint 1) 2)
Customer ID Security Pin
Date Note

Website
Username
Email
Password
Password Update
Password Update
Password Hint 1) 2)
Customer ID Security Pin
Date Note

U

Website

Username

Email

Password

Password Update

Password Update

Password Hint 1) 2)

Customer ID Security Pin

Date Note

Website

Username

Email

Password

Password Update

Password Update

Password Hint 1) 2)

Customer ID Security Pin

Date Note

Website

Username

Email

Password

Password Update

Password Update

Password Hint 1) 2)

Customer ID Security Pin

Date Note

"But now faith, hope, love, abide these three; but the greatest of these is love."

1 Corinthians 13:13

Website
Username
Email
Password
Password Update
Password Update
Password Hint 1) 2)
Customer ID Security Pin
Date Note

Website
Username
Email
Password
Password Update
Password Update
Password Hint 1) 2)
Customer ID Security Pin
Date Note

Website
Username
Email
Password
Password Update
Password Update
Password Hint 1) 2)
Customer ID Security Pin
Date Note

V

Website

Username

Email

Password

Password Update

Password Update

Password Hint 1) 2)

Customer ID Security Pin

Date Note

Website

Username

Email

Password

Password Update

Password Update

Password Hint 1) 2)

Customer ID Security Pin

Date Note

Website

Username

Email

Password

Password Update

Password Update

Password Hint 1) 2)

Customer ID Security Pin

Date Note

Website
Username
Email
Password
Password Update
Password Update
Password Hint 1) 2)
Customer ID Security Pin
Date Note

Website
Username
Email
Password
Password Update
Password Update
Password Hint 1) 2)
Customer ID Security Pin
Date Note

Website
Username
Email
Password
Password Update
Password Update
Password Hint 1) 2)
Customer ID Security Pin
Date Note

V

Website

Username

Email

Password

Password Update

Password Update

Password Hint 1) 2)

Customer ID Security Pin

Date Note

Website

Username

Email

Password

Password Update

Password Update

Password Hint 1) 2)

Customer ID Security Pin

Date Note

Website

Username

Email

Password

Password Update

Password Update

Password Hint 1) 2)

Customer ID Security Pin

Date Note

V

Website
Username
Email
Password
Password Update
Password Update
Password Hint 1) 2)
Customer ID Security Pin
Date Note

Website
Username
Email
Password
Password Update
Password Update
Password Hint 1) 2)
Customer ID Security Pin
Date Note

Website
Username
Email
Password
Password Update
Password Update
Password Hint 1) 2)
Customer ID Security Pin
Date Note

V

Website

Username

Email

Password

Password Update

Password Update

Password Hint 1) 2)

Customer ID Security Pin

Date Note

Website

Username

Email

Password

Password Update

Password Update

Password Hint 1) 2)

Customer ID Security Pin

Date Note

Website

Username

Email

Password

Password Update

Password Update

Password Hint 1) 2)

Customer ID Security Pin

Date Note

"Come, you who are blessed of My Father,
inherit the kingdom prepared for you
from the foundation of the world."

Matthew 25:34

W

Website

Username

Email

Password

Password Update

Password Update

Password Hint 1) 2)

Customer ID Security Pin

Date Note

Website

Username

Email

Password

Password Update

Password Update

Password Hint 1) 2)

Customer ID Security Pin

Date Note

Website

Username

Email

Password

Password Update

Password Update

Password Hint 1) 2)

Customer ID Security Pin

Date Note

W

Website

Username

Email

Password

Password Update

Password Update

Password Hint 1) 2)

Customer ID Security Pin

Date Note

Website

Username

Email

Password

Password Update

Password Update

Password Hint 1) 2)

Customer ID Security Pin

Date Note

Website

Username

Email

Password

Password Update

Password Update

Password Hint 1) 2)

Customer ID Security Pin

Date Note

Website

Username

Email

Password

Password Update

Password Update

Password Hint 1) 2)

Customer ID Security Pin

Date Note

Website

Username

Email

Password

Password Update

Password Update

Password Hint 1) 2)

Customer ID Security Pin

Date Note

Website

Username

Email

Password

Password Update

Password Update

Password Hint 1) 2)

Customer ID Security Pin

Date Note

W

Website

Username

Email

Password

Password Update

Password Update

Password Hint 1) 2)

Customer ID Security Pin

Date Note

Website

Username

Email

Password

Password Update

Password Update

Password Hint 1) 2)

Customer ID Security Pin

Date Note

Website

Username

Email

Password

Password Update

Password Update

Password Hint 1) 2)

Customer ID Security Pin

Date Note

Website
Username
Email
Password
Password Update
Password Update
Password Hint 1) 2)
Customer ID Security Pin
Date Note

Website
Username
Email
Password
Password Update
Password Update
Password Hint 1) 2)
Customer ID Security Pin
Date Note

Website
Username
Email
Password
Password Update
Password Update
Password Hint 1) 2)
Customer ID Security Pin
Date Note

W

Website
Username
Email
Password
Password Update
Password Update
Password Hint 1) 2)
Customer ID Security Pin
Date Note

Website
Username
Email
Password
Password Update
Password Update
Password Hint 1) 2)
Customer ID Security Pin
Date Note

Website
Username
Email
Password
Password Update
Password Update
Password Hint 1) 2)
Customer ID Security Pin
Date Note

"For I was hungry, and you gave Me something to eat; I was thirsty, and you gave Me something to drink; I was a stranger, and you invited Me in; naked, and you clothed Me; I was sick, and you visited Me; I was in prison, and you came to Me."

Matthew 25:35-36

Website
Username
Email
Password
Password Update
Password Update
Password Hint 1) 2)
Customer ID Security Pin
Date Note

Website
Username
Email
Password
Password Update
Password Update
Password Hint 1) 2)
Customer ID Security Pin
Date Note

Website
Username
Email
Password
Password Update
Password Update
Password Hint 1) 2)
Customer ID Security Pin
Date Note

X

Website
Username
Email
Password
Password Update
Password Update
Password Hint 1) 2)
Customer ID Security Pin
Date Note

Website
Username
Email
Password
Password Update
Password Update
Password Hint 1) 2)
Customer ID Security Pin
Date Note

Website
Username
Email
Password
Password Update
Password Update
Password Hint 1) 2)
Customer ID Security Pin
Date Note

Website

Username

Email

Password

Password Update

Password Update

Password Hint 1) 2)

Customer ID Security Pin

Date Note

Website

Username

Email

Password

Password Update

Password Update

Password Hint 1) 2)

Customer ID Security Pin

Date Note

Website

Username

Email

Password

Password Update

Password Update

Password Hint 1) 2)

Customer ID Security Pin

Date Note

X

Website

Username

Email

Password

Password Update

Password Update

Password Hint 1) 2)

Customer ID Security Pin

Date Note

Website

Username

Email

Password

Password Update

Password Update

Password Hint 1) 2)

Customer ID Security Pin

Date Note

Website

Username

Email

Password

Password Update

Password Update

Password Hint 1) 2)

Customer ID Security Pin

Date Note

Website

Username

Email

Password

Password Update

Password Update

Password Hint 1) 2)

Customer ID Security Pin

Date Note

Website

Username

Email

Password

Password Update

Password Update

Password Hint 1) 2)

Customer ID Security Pin

Date Note

Website

Username

Email

Password

Password Update

Password Update

Password Hint 1) 2)

Customer ID Security Pin

Date Note

X

Website

Username

Email

Password

Password Update

Password Update

Password Hint 1) 2)

Customer ID Security Pin

Date Note

Website

Username

Email

Password

Password Update

Password Update

Password Hint 1) 2)

Customer ID Security Pin

Date Note

Website

Username

Email

Password

Password Update

Password Update

Password Hint 1) 2)

Customer ID Security Pin

Date Note

"Then the righteous will answer Him, 'Lord, when did we see You hungry, and feed You, or thirsty, and give You something to drink? And when did we see You a stranger, and invite You in, or naked, and clothe You? When did we see You sick, or in prison, and come to You?'"

Matthew 25:37-39

Website
Username
Email
Password
Password Update
Password Update
Password Hint 1) 2)
Customer ID Security Pin
Date Note

Website
Username
Email
Password
Password Update
Password Update
Password Hint 1) 2)
Customer ID Security Pin
Date Note

Website
Username
Email
Password
Password Update
Password Update
Password Hint 1) 2)
Customer ID Security Pin
Date Note

Y

Website

Username

Email

Password

Password Update

Password Update

Password Hint 1) 2)

Customer ID Security Pin

Date Note

Website

Username

Email

Password

Password Update

Password Update

Password Hint 1) 2)

Customer ID Security Pin

Date Note

Website

Username

Email

Password

Password Update

Password Update

Password Hint 1) 2)

Customer ID Security Pin

Date Note

Website
Username
Email
Password
Password Update
Password Update
Password Hint 1) 2)
Customer ID Security Pin
Date Note

Website
Username
Email
Password
Password Update
Password Update
Password Hint 1) 2)
Customer ID Security Pin
Date Note

Website
Username
Email
Password
Password Update
Password Update
Password Hint 1) 2)
Customer ID Security Pin
Date Note

Y

Website

Username

Email

Password

Password Update

Password Update

Password Hint 1) 2)

Customer ID Security Pin

Date Note

Website

Username

Email

Password

Password Update

Password Update

Password Hint 1) 2)

Customer ID Security Pin

Date Note

Website

Username

Email

Password

Password Update

Password Update

Password Hint 1) 2)

Customer ID Security Pin

Date Note

Y

Website
Username
Email
Password
Password Update
Password Update
Password Hint 1) 2)
Customer ID Security Pin
Date Note

Website
Username
Email
Password
Password Update
Password Update
Password Hint 1) 2)
Customer ID Security Pin
Date Note

Website
Username
Email
Password
Password Update
Password Update
Password Hint 1) 2)
Customer ID Security Pin
Date Note

Y

Website

Username

Email

Password

Password Update

Password Update

Password Hint 1) 2)

Customer ID Security Pin

Date Note

Website

Username

Email

Password

Password Update

Password Update

Password Hint 1) 2)

Customer ID Security Pin

Date Note

Website

Username

Email

Password

Password Update

Password Update

Password Hint 1) 2)

Customer ID Security Pin

Date Note

"The King will answer and say to them, 'Truly I say to you, to the extent that you did it to one of these brothers of Mine, even the least of them, you did it to Me.'"

Matthew 25:40

Website
Username
Email
Password
Password Update
Password Update
Password Hint 1) 2)
Customer ID Security Pin
Date Note

Website
Username
Email
Password
Password Update
Password Update
Password Hint 1) 2)
Customer ID Security Pin
Date Note

Website
Username
Email
Password
Password Update
Password Update
Password Hint 1) 2)
Customer ID Security Pin
Date Note

Z

Website

Username

Email

Password

Password Update

Password Update

Password Hint 1) 2)

Customer ID Security Pin

Date Note

Website

Username

Email

Password

Password Update

Password Update

Password Hint 1) 2)

Customer ID Security Pin

Date Note

Website

Username

Email

Password

Password Update

Password Update

Password Hint 1) 2)

Customer ID Security Pin

Date Note

Z

Website

Username

Email

Password

Password Update

Password Update

Password Hint 1) 2)

Customer ID Security Pin

Date Note

Website

Username

Email

Password

Password Update

Password Update

Password Hint 1) 2)

Customer ID Security Pin

Date Note

Website

Username

Email

Password

Password Update

Password Update

Password Hint 1) 2)

Customer ID Security Pin

Date Note

Z

Website

Username

Email

Password

Password Update

Password Update

Password Hint 1) 2)

Customer ID Security Pin

Date Note

Website

Username

Email

Password

Password Update

Password Update

Password Hint 1) 2)

Customer ID Security Pin

Date Note

Website

Username

Email

Password

Password Update

Password Update

Password Hint 1) 2)

Customer ID Security Pin

Date Note

Website

Username

Email

Password

Password Update

Password Update

Password Hint 1) 2)

Customer ID Security Pin

Date Note

Website

Username

Email

Password

Password Update

Password Update

Password Hint 1) 2)

Customer ID Security Pin

Date Note

Website

Username

Email

Password

Password Update

Password Update

Password Hint 1) 2)

Customer ID Security Pin

Date Note

Z

Website

Username

Email

Password

Password Update

Password Update

Password Hint 1) 2)

Customer ID Security Pin

Date Note

Website

Username

Email

Password

Password Update

Password Update

Password Hint 1) 2)

Customer ID Security Pin

Date Note

Website

Username

Email

Password

Password Update

Password Update

Password Hint 1) 2)

Customer ID Security Pin

Date Note

"Do not be afraid any longer, only believe."

Mark 5:36

A Note from the Author

Have you ever wondered if you matter to God?

I want you to know, you are not alone. God is with you. And so am I.

I may not know you, but I am praying for you.

The Lord gave us each other so that we may comfort one another as we make our way through this epic journey called life.

Look beyond the world you see to find God in the world not seen with eyes, but with your heart.

In time, the unseen world will become visible, once the light of this world fades behind us.

May the Lord lift you up, set your feet upon a rock and give you His peace which surpasses all understanding.

Jeff Silvius

"In the world you have tribulation,
but take courage;
I have overcome the world."

John 16:33

Made in United States
North Haven, CT
05 November 2026

21767244R00128